W9-APT-348

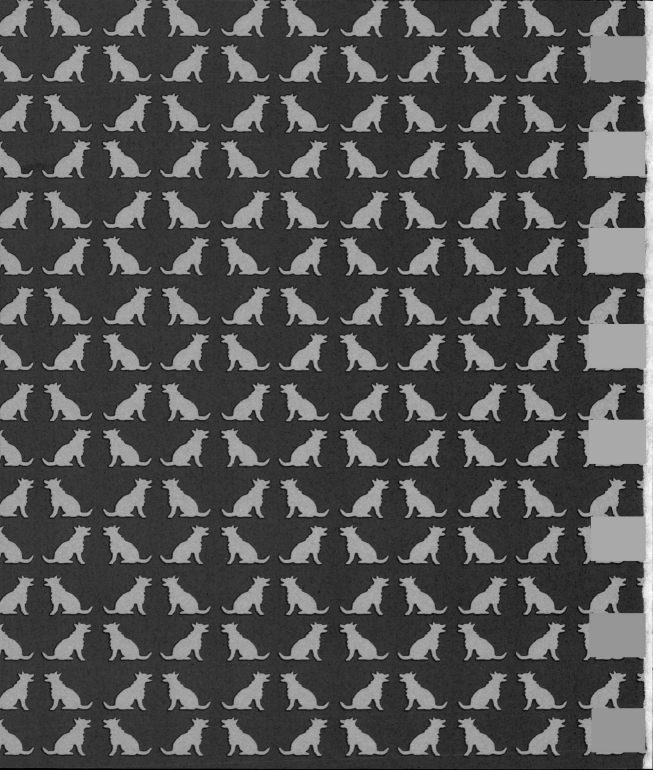

DOG TALES

DOG TALES

CLASSIC STORIES ABOUT SMART DOGS

WITH PHOTOGRAPHS BY MYRON BECK

INTRODUCTION BY RICHARD A. WOLTERS

WINGS BOOKS
New York

Grateful acknowledgment is made for permission to reprint the following copyrighted works:
"Your Boy and His Dog" from *Chips Off the Old Benchley* by Robert Benchley. Copyright 1949 By Gertrude D. Benchley. Reprinted by
permission of Harper & Row, Publishers, Inc.
"MacDunald" from John Held, Jr.'s *Dog Stories.* Copyright 1930 by the Vanguard Press, Inc. Reprinted by permission of Vanguard Press,
a division of Random House, Inc.
"Lassie Come Home" by Eric Knight. Copyright 1938 by The Curtis Publishing Company. Copyright renewed 1966 by Jere Knight,
Betty Noyes Knight, Winifred Knight Mewborn, and Jennie Knight Moore. Reprinted by permission of Curtis Brown, Ltd.
"Dogs" from *First and Last* by Ring Lardner. Reprinted by permission of Charles Scribner's Sons, an imprint of Macmillan Publishing
Company. Copyright 1934 by Ellis A. Lardner; renewal copyright © 1962 by Ring Lardner, Jr.
"Toward the Dog Days" from *Here Are Dogs* by Dorothy Parker. Copyright 1931 by Dorothy Parker. Reprinted by permission of the NAACP,
agents for the literary estate of Dorothy Parker.
"Louis" from *The Complete Short Stories of Saki* (H. H. Munro). Copyright 1930, renewed © 1958 by The Viking Press, Inc. Reprinted by
permission of Viking Penguin, a division of Penguin Books USA Inc.
"The Dog That Bit People" from *My Life and Hard Times* by James Thurber, published by Harper & Row. Reprinted by permission of
Rosemary A. Thurber and Hamish Hamilton Ltd. Copyright © 1933, 1961 by James Thurber.

This 1996 edition is published by Wings Books, a division of Random House Value Publishing, Inc., 201 East 50th Street, New York 10022,
by arrangement with Studio Books, a division of Penguin Books USA, Inc.

Wings Books and colophon are trademarks of Random House Value Publishing, Inc.

Random House
New York • Toronto • London • Sydney • Auckland
http://www.randomhouse.com/

Printed and bound in China

Library of Congress Cataloging-in-Publication Data
Dog tales : classic stories about smart dogs / with photographs by Myron Beck ; introduction by Richard A. Wolters.
        p.   cm.
     Contents: Your boy and his dog / Robert Benchley—MacDunald / John Held, Jr.—Memories of a yellow dog / O. Henry—Lassie come
home / Eric Night—Dogs / Ring Lardner—Being a public character / Don Marquis—Toward the dog days / Dorothy Parker—Louis /
Saki—The dog that bit people / James Thurber.
   ISBN 0-517-14855-2
   1. Dogs—Fiction. 2. Human-animal relationships—Fiction. 3. Short stories, American. I. Beck, Myron.
  [PS648.D64D64   1996]   95-41613
  813'.010836—dc20   CIP

8   7   6   5   4   3

To Irwin and Leona Beck
and
Harvey and Shirley Thornby

My partner Kirk Thornby and I wish to give a special thank you to Rita Aero and Esther Mitgang who conceived the original idea for this wonderful project. Their support and enthusiasm provided a great environment in which our work could flourish. We also thank Stephanie Gibbons and the Golden Rule Kennels, who found the perfect dogs for every shot, and with Bobby, stuck it out each day to the end. A sincere thank you to Brian Toffoli for his great ideas, creativity, and enthusiasm; and to Karen Oliver, who did a great job. We'd also like to thank AIM color lab, Kai Jorgensen, and David Pelon for their helping hands.

Grateful thanks to the dogs and their owners: Ann Boardman's Saint Bernard, Love; Margaret and Anne Spinella's English bulldog, Bee Jay, Tuff-Haven Kennels; Ken and Nancy Hall's English springer spaniel, Jesy, Marjon Kennels; Marilu Tiberi-Vipraio's basset hound, Tubby; Cyndi Varner's Airedale terrier, Katie, Coppercrest Kennels; Loretta Allen's collie, Paddy Too; Judy Chard's Australian shepherd, Dash, Casa Blanca Kennels; Debbie Perrot's petit basset Griffon Vendeen, Flyer, and German wire-haired pointer, Tic Tac Toe, Hootwire Kennels; Susan Porter's West Highland white terrier, Douglas, Evermore Kennels; Maxine Martin's Great Pyrenees, Ringo, Shadowrun Kennels; Doty Ambrose's beagles, Daphne and Toby, Woodhill Kennels; Martha Merrill's Scottish terrier, Wheatie, Merrilland Kennels; Dr. and Mrs. Steven Williams' shar-pei, Elliot; Ken and Toni Gibson's dalmatian, Spotslight Lord Murphy; Stephanie and Jim Gibbons' golden retriever, Rhett, Golden Rule Kennels; Peggy Boltz and Robert Giamo's mastiff, Guido; Elisa Leone's Siberian husky/malamute, Kuya; Kathryn Segura's Shetland sheepdogs, Tasha and Tiffany; and Gay Del Duca's calico cat, Jezebel.

Page 13: English tack courtesy of Eland Ranch, Chino, California.
Page 23: Green bench courtesy of Mandy's Antiques.
Page 73: Linens courtesy of Lexington Place, Pasadena, California; pillows courtesy of Mandy's Antiques, Sherman Oaks, California.

CONTENTS

INTRODUCTION   BY

RICHARD A. WOLTERS

Now that you've taken *Dog Tales* off the shelf we know this much: you're a "dog peo-ple." Don't just stand there holding it, do something … buy it … borrow it … swipe it. Look what we've got … luminaries such as Robert Benchley, O. Henry, Eric Knight, Ring Lardner, Dorothy Parker, and James Thurber. They're among the best storytellers of this century.

I've sold almost a million copies of my hunting-dog books, but after reading the sto-ries in this book I realize that I've failed my own Labradors. Tar, who is better-known than I am, and can attract more pretty ladies than I can, has been named for the last three years to the list of the top thirty hunting retrievers in the country. But I hate to admit it: he can't read or write a word.

Tar's education won't be complete until he learns, as in Don Marquis's story, "Being a Public Character," how to be a hero and bite a lion or save babies in a fire. In Benchley's story "Your Boy and His Dog," the dog, it's suggested, because of his wisdom, should run for president. My dog Tar could only be elected garbage collector. Eric Knight's story "Lassie Come Home" could teach Tar to find his way, over five hundred miles, back to me. Instead, I have to go fetch Tar if he runs two hundreds yards from my front door.

James Thurber had a great dog, Muggs, who learned how to bite people. Tar thinks his teeth are meant only for eating chocolate. Thurber writes, "There was a slight advantage in being one of the family, for [Muggs] didn't bite family as often as he bit strangers. Still, in the years we had him, he bit everyone but Mother, and he made a pass at her once but missed." Oh, Tar, when our house was robbed why did you invite the crook in, lick his face, and show him where the silver was hidden?

The stories, classic literature, are only part of this book! Look at the photographs by Myron Beck. Tar's education is lacking another way. He wouldn't know a good picture from a snapshot, but I would because I was the first picture editor of *Sports Illustrated*. Myron Beck's pictures set the scene well for this collection of writing celebrities.

Study these canine portraits carefully. Play a game … it's sort of a doggie Rorschach test. I've found my local banker, eccentric Aunt Minnie, and lovable Dr. Heckman. There's Miss Harmon, my nasty second-grade teacher; the cop on the corner who gave me a ticket; Rebecca, my sixth-grade love; the bully who beat me up in the school yard; and wrinkle-faced Dr. Willard, my college chemistry professor. I even saw Muggs, who looks like what I think James Thurber looked like. *You do it* ... you play the game. You too might find some people you loved, feared, hated, respected, and some you wanted to forget.

I'm sorry the black Labrador is not in these pictures. That is my real grown-up love. Do you know that Tar, who does not think he's a person, as most of the dogs in these stories do, does some remarkable stuff in spite of his not even knowing the alphabet?

Try this story! If Tar is sitting on the floor of my duck blind, and a bird is wounded, from where he sits he will not see it go down or know where it is. Even if it sails off two hundred yards, Tar, as a real conservationist, will without fail retrieve that duck. By law, if the bird is not recovered, the hunter may shoot another ... a terrible waste. Tar and I are a team. I'll sit him at heel outside the duck blind. With my hand in front of his face, I'll show him the direction I saw the bird go down, then command him to swim that course as straight as an arrow. If he gets off path, I'll stop him with my whistle. He'll turn, doggie-paddle, and look at me for instructions. My arm signal shows him the way, then he'll take the new direction. I can stop him as often as needed to correct his line to the duck, which may now be hundreds of yards away hiding in the reeds. When he's close enough to pick up the scent of the bird, he'll make the retrieve, then he'll carry the duck back to me with nary as much as a wrinkled feather.

Okay, Thurber, Benchley, O. Henry, Dorothy Parker, and especially you, Ring Lardner (the great sportswriter of your day), could your dogs do that? Tar won't be president, or bite lions, crooks, or Mother, but he ain't so dumb after all.

Read *Dog Tales*. It's fun! Even Tar's enjoying it. . . . Well, anyway, he likes the pictures.

YOUR BOY AND HIS DOG

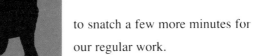

People are constantly asking me: "What kind of dog shall I give my boy?" or sometimes: "What kind of boy shall I give my dog?" And although we are always somewhat surprised to get a query like this, ours really being the Jam and Fern Question Box, we usually give the same answer to both forms of inquiry: "Are you quite sure that you want to do either?" This confuses them, and we are able to snatch a few more minutes for our regular work.

But the question of Boy and Dog is one which will not be downed. There is no doubt that every healthy, normal boy (if there is such a thing in these days of Child Study) should own a dog at some time in his life, preferably between the ages of forty-five and fifty. Give a dog to a boy who is much younger and his parents will find

BENCHLEY

themselves obliged to pack up and go to the Sailors' Snug Harbor to live until the dog runs away — which he will do as soon as the first pretty face comes along.

But a dog teaches a boy fidelity, perseverance, and to turn around three times before lying down — very important traits in times like these. In fact, just as soon as a dog comes along who, in addition to these qualities, also knows when to buy and sell stocks, he can be moved right up to the boy's bedroom and the boy can sleep in the dog house.

In buying a dog for a very small child, attention must be paid to one or two essential points. In the first place, the dog must be one which will come apart easily or of such a breed that the sizing will get pasty and all gummed up when wet. Dachshunds are ideal dogs for small children, as they are already stretched and pulled to such a length that the child cannot do much harm one way or the other. The dachshund being so long also makes it difficult for a very small child to go through with the favorite juvenile maneuver of lifting the dog's hind legs up in the air and wheeling it along like a barrow, cooing, "Diddy-ap!" Any small child trying to lift a dachshund's hind legs up very high is going to find itself flat on its back.

For the very small child who likes to pick animals up around the middle and carry them over to the fireplace, mastiffs, St. Bernards, or Russian wolfhounds are not indicated — that is, not if the child is of any value at all. It is not that the larger dogs resent being carried around the middle and dropped in the fireplace (in fact, the smaller the dog, the more touchy it is in matters of dignity, as is so often the case with people and nations); but, even though a mastiff does everything that it can to help the child in carrying it by the diaphragm, there are matters of gravity to be reckoned with which make it impossible to carry the thing through without something being broken. If a dog could be trained to wrestle and throw the child immediately, a great deal of time could be saved.

But, as we have suggested, the ideal age for a boy to own a dog is between forty-five and fifty. By this time the boy ought to have attained his full growth and, provided he is ever going to, ought to know more or less what he wants to make of himself in life. At this age the dog will be more of a companion than a chattel, and, if necessary, can be counted upon to carry the boy by the middle and drop him into bed in case sleep overcomes him at a dinner or camp meeting or anything. It can also be counted upon to tell him he has made a fool of himself and embarrassed all his friends. A wife could do no more.

The training of the dog is something which should be left to the boy, as this teaches him responsibility and accustoms him to the use of authority, probably the only time he will ever have a chance to use it. If, for example, the dog insists on following the boy when he is leaving the house, even after repeated commands to "Go on back home!" the boy must decide on one of two courses. He must either take the dog back to the house and lock it in the cellar, or, as an alternate course, he can give up the idea of going out himself and stay with the dog. The latter is the better way, especially if the dog is in good voice and given to screaming the house down.

There has always been considerable difference of opinion as to whether or not a dog really thinks. I, personally, have no doubt that distinct mental processes do go on inside the dog's brain, although many times these processes are hardly worthy of the name. I have known dogs, especially puppies, who were almost as stupid as humans in their mental reactions.

The only reason that puppies do not get into more trouble than they do (if there *is* any more trouble than that which puppies get into) is that they are so small. A child, for instance, should not expect to be able to fall as heavily, eat as heartily of shoe leather, or throw up as casually as a puppy does, for there is more bulk to a child and the results of these practices will be

more serious in exact proportion to the size and capacity. Whereas, for example, a puppy might be able to eat only the toe of a slipper, a child might well succeed in eating the whole shoe — which, considering the nails and everything, would not be wise.

One of the reasons why dogs are given credit for serious thinking is the formation of their eyebrows. A dog lying in front of a fire and looking up at his master may appear pathetic, disapproving, sage, or amused, according to the angle at which its eyebrows are set by nature.

It is quite possible, and even probable, that nothing at all is going on behind the eyebrows. In fact, one dog who had a great reputation for sagacity once told me in confidence that most of the time when he was supposed to be regarding a human with an age-old philosophical rumination he was really asleep behind his shaggy overhanging brows. "You could have knocked me over with a feather," he said, "when I found out that people were talking about my wisdom and suggesting running me for President."

This, of course, offers a possibility for the future of the child itself. As soon as the boy makes up his mind just what type of man he wants to be, he could buy some crêpe hair and a bottle of spirit gum and make himself a pair of eyebrows to suit the rôle: converging toward the nose if he wants to be a judge or savant; pointing upward from the edge of the eyes if he wants to be a worried-looking man, like a broker; elevated to his forehead if he plans on simulating surprise as a personal characteristic; and in red patches if he intends being a stage Irishman.

In this way he may be able to get away with a great deal, as his pal the dog does.

At any rate, the important thing is to get a dog for the boy and see what each can teach the other. The way things are going now with our Younger Generation, the chances are that before long the dog will be smoking, drinking gin, and wearing a soft hat pulled over one eye.

MACDUNALD

My name is MacDunald, and I'm as braw a Scot as ever chewed up a pair of slippers. I'm stubborn and I'm canny, I'm short-legged and close to the ground, what I lack in size I make up in courage. The Scotch are a fighting race and the Tartar of my clan has never dragged the dust, my breed has never known defeat and we die game, do we Scots. My hair is coarse and wiry and my tail is carried high. I want to tell you these facts so you won't think me a sissy even if I do live a soft life in a fashionable neighborhood.

I make my home with a nice pair of folks. I'm very fond of my folks, very fond. I could run away if I wanted to, but I have no desire to leave. My folks treat me well. Sometimes things don't go just as I plan, but a dog must expect to put up with some disa-

HELD

HELD

greeable things, so I suppose I'm as well off as most of the dogs that I know.

My man treats me like an equal, that's all I ask of him. My woman wants to baby me sometimes, but I overlook that, because she has no children of her own, and she has the need to mother something. But I understand, and I allow her to vent her maternal urge up to a certain point — when it gets too thick I can always go and hide under the bed. Sometimes it gets me nervous when women get too motherly with me. I'm pretty salty myself so I always stay outdoors when my woman has her girl friends in to play bridge, afternoons. Of course I'm fond of bits of cinnamon toast and a lump of sugar now and then, but these women always want to talk baby talk and stuff me with food, and a dog needs to watch or he'll get fat and out of condition.

I don't want to get soft and not be able to keep myself in fighting trim, because there are a lot of snooty dogs out in our subdivision that might need to be whipped some day, so you see I have to stay in training. So far, I haven't had to punish one of them, but you never know when one of those stupid Police dogs will need to be put in his place. Just let one of them come around and try to smell one of my bushes or shrubs, then they will hear the bagpipes.

You can stop listening now if I am boring you, because I know what it is to be bored and have to listen to something that doesn't interest me, like when my woman used to read to me. But I mustn't criticize my woman. She is a good sort. We spend a great deal of time together, and get on rather well, but I could do without having those stories read to me. I always made out as if I was interested when she used to read those silly stories to me about Collies when we were all alone evenings, when my man would telephone and say he was detained at the office or was at the Club or was entertaining customers, or whatever he really was doing. Of course, in the first place I have a contempt for what call themselves Scotch Collies, a silken-

coated, narrow-minded breed. Scotch, indeed, and always doing something human in the stories — disgusting, I say. Makes me feel like I did when I ate the dozen cream-puffs. Stories about Collies that have been bred for bench shows, not the good old Shepherd dog of Scotland. Ah, there was a dog that should have been a Terrier. A dog that knew his work and did it. How could a man manage sheep if he didn't have a dog that had brains? My woman takes me out a great deal. I like it when we motor out to the Country Club. Of course I'd like it better if she would allow me to chase the golf balls. I remember one afternoon when she didn't watch me I went out and had sport; altogether I got seven golf balls and buried them and then sat back in the grass and listened to the players swear and rave because they couldn't find the balls. That was a good afternoon.

I like it when we go over to the Hunt Club and I can go and sniff around the stables. There are some lovely places to roll. The only drawback to that is, my woman always insists on giving me a bath when we get home and I hate the soap she uses. It takes days to get rid of that odor and get to smelling like a dog again. Imagine trying to threaten an Airedale or a Schnauzer if you smell of jasmine. It's things like that, that make life difficult for a dog. But if I intend to keep my folks I'll have to concede some of my dislikes and blame it on the civilization that we live in.

There is another place where I always have a good time. That's out in the country on my woman's father's farm. He likes to call it a farm, but my woman always calls it an expense, and says it's a good thing that her father is wealthy, otherwise he couldn't afford to be a farmer. But it's nice out there to chase rats in the granary and bark at and worry the calves. I enjoy sitting on the sunny side of the silo and gossiping with my old friend the Pointer. He likes to tell me the good times he and the old gentleman used to have when they went

HELD

shooting. He loves to boast about all the good points he used to make and how he used to be able to hold quail in any cover. He's too old to go out hunting any more. His hind quarters are all tightened up with rheumatism. He must have had a full life and now he likes to sit and talk about it.

It must be satisfying to know you have always done your work well, like the old Pointer does. I'm not much of a sporting dog myself, although I would like to get a chance to dig out a rabbit, but I'm better at amusing my folks. That's the best thing I do and I think a dog always should do the thing he does best.

I've got one or two pretty good tricks and they always seem to work. My best trick is to go out every morning and get the mail from the postman. He comes up to our path and blows his whistle for me and I run out and bring in the letters. My other trick is to just sit down and move my head from side to side — that always gets a big laugh. I tried another trick once but it didn't seem to get over very well and oh, what a spanking I got. I figured out that my man wasn't so pleased with the part of the newspaper that printed long lists of stock reports — it was something about the markets, as I understand it. One morning I thought it would be a good trick to fix that page, so I went out and got the paper first and chewed that page up to bits, and as I said, I got spanked for that trick. I never tried it again. That's the only time I ever was punished.

My woman has never so much as raised a hand to me. Sometimes she scolds, but I pay no attention to that, and my man only did it once, but he didn't feel so good that morning. There had been a party the night before, and my folks move in a hard-drinking set. In fact all the Country Club folks are heavy drinkers. I like the smell of Scotch whiskey. I suppose I inherit that. I love to get into my man's room and sleep on his tweeds, they smell of tobacco and

11

HELD

liquor like a man's clothes should smell. He's a dog's man and no mistake.

Speaking of parties, there have been some rather lively ones at our house. I always get put upstairs when I try to sing in with the guests, but I get to see a lot because they never start to sing until the party is well under way. There seems to be more parties than there used to be, nearly every night now. If the crowd don't come to our house my folks go out to other places.

They leave me to watch the house until they get back. I like the responsibility, and I'd like to see any stranger get into the house when I am here alone — I'd make short work of them. Sometimes I begin to wonder if my folks are ever going to get home, sometimes it's daylight before they get in, and I'm pretty sleepy after keeping on guard all night.

I wish my woman didn't have to drive the car when she brings my man home. She isn't a very good driver, she's not a bad driver, mind you, but she isn't as expert as my man. And after those parties I miss the morning walk we used to take, but my man is not equal to a walk the morning after. He just gets up and doesn't say much, then he goes and catches a train and my woman and I are alone all day, except when all the other dogs' women come in for bridge and cocktails, or else the Artist fellow comes in for tea.

I don't like him very well, he tries to act like my man used to when he is with my woman, but my man doesn't act that way any more and I suppose my woman wants some man to act that way. Women are like that, and men are like that, always in love. I'm different, I only get in love twice a year, I think that's plenty. My man was very much in love with my woman a while back but he doesn't talk about it any more. I don't see why, as my woman is very pretty, as women go. She has nice dark eyes and her hands are soft. I think she is still very much in love with my man, because she is always telling the Artist that he mustn't talk that way. Then she makes him go away, and after he's gone she cries and that's the time I always

HELD

try to amuse her with my head-tilting trick.

Once after the Artist had gone I went and got one of my man's old hats and fetched it to her, but that made her cry and she went into her room and shut the door, so I went downstairs and waited for my man to come home but he didn't come home that night and didn't telephone either.

Next day I heard that he had to go to Atlantic City with a customer and he was gone ten days. While he was away my woman took me to the Artist's Studio where he was painting a picture of her. I didn't think it was a very good picture of her, but then I don't know anything about art. I didn't think he was very interested in this painting, as all he wanted to do was sit and look into my woman's dark eyes. He just stared at her because she wouldn't let him talk about love. Then he made out as if he was hurt and got up and painted some more. I didn't like it at the Artist's Studio. It smelled of paint and turpentine and some sickening thing he burned to make smoke. I think they call it incense. It was terrible and made me cough. I can't quite figure my woman out when she goes to the Artist's place. She is so careful when she dresses to go there. She puts on her softest things and fixes herself up beautiful. Sometimes I think she likes to have the Artist tell her how lovely she is. I don't think that is right, it's too much like the people who come to our house to the parties. The men are always telling other men's wives how much they like them. I know because I hear and see things. Nobody pays any attention to me. Many times I'm upstairs napping when the noise gets on my nerves and the men and women slip into the dark room and make love. They don't seem to mind if I see them. I hate to see my woman get that way with this Artist. But I suppose my woman is unhappy if she hasn't got someone to love her. That's why she comes to the studio and has the Artist over for tea when my man doesn't come home.

14

HELD

I wish my folks would spend the evenings like they did when we first came to live at our house. Those were pleasant times. We would have a good fire and they would sit and talk about love and then we would go to the kitchen and have a snack before we retired. I enjoyed those snacks. You know a dog gets hungry in the evening. But now whenever my man comes home they either have a drinking party at the house with people in, or else they go out and come in late. They never seem to talk much to each other.

My woman stopped going to the Artist's Studio after what I did. It's odd too, she didn't even scold me. I took a bite at that Artist. I can still taste the turpentine. That afternoon we went over there, my woman had a strange look in her eyes. The Artist didn't paint much. He started right in to talk about love and how he couldn't stand it any longer, and my woman didn't stop him. She just let him rave. Then the Artist went over to my woman and took her in his arms and kissed her. She didn't seem to mind it so I growled and bit him. Then he swore at me and my woman got into her coat and we went right home. She never went back there for her picture. It wasn't a good picture anyway.

The Artist telephoned to her but she always told the maid to say she wasn't in. She told me afterwards, "Mac, you saved me from doing something terrible." As I said before, I'm a canny Scot. She never said anything about the Artist business to my man.

Then my man started to come home evenings again, but those evenings were pretty dull. He would eat his dinner and then he would sit and read the stock reports for a while, then he would say: "I have a hard day tomorrow, I think I'll turn in." And up he would get and go to bed and sleep in his own room. I would see my woman's lights burning late as I went about the house checking everything up before I went down to sleep myself.

It's funny how things happen, isn't it? The other morning I saw a chance to do one of my

HELD

tricks. I thought perhaps it would cheer my woman up a bit. It was after we had eaten breakfast and my man had rushed to his train. I went out to listen for the postman's whistle but I guess I must have missed hearing it, because there on the path was a letter. I went out and got it and fetched it in and gave it to my woman. It was a queer sort of letter; it smelled of a kind of perfume that one of my woman's girl friends always uses, and it wasn't sealed up like the other letters. My woman took the paper out of the envelope and read it. Then she just stood and looked strange. An odd hard look came into her eyes, then she went and called the Artist on the telephone. After that she went up to her room and packed a bag. Then she came down and wrote a note and took it in my man's room and stuck it in the edge of his shaving mirror. She put the bag in the car and drove away, without saying good-bye to me.

I stayed close to the house all that day. It's a good thing I did because a new dog came down our street and I had to inform him that he must keep off my place.

When my man came home I tried to get him to go up and get the note but he just went into all the rooms looking for my woman. The maid was off that day. Finally he found the note in his shaving mirror and after he had read it he just sat down and stared ahead of him for a while, then he said to me: "Mac, old boy, you should always remember to tear up certain kinds of correspondence." Then he took a bath and changed his clothes and packed a bag. He put me on a leash and we walked down to a boarding kennel and asked the kennel man if he could look out for me for a few days. The kennel man said "yes." So here I am.

I wish I knew what it was all about. I don't like it here. Perhaps it is all for the best, because I might need to bite the Artist again.

MEMOIRS OF
A YELLOW DOG

I don't suppose it will knock any of you people off your perch to read a contribution from an animal. Mr. Kipling and a good many others have demonstrated the fact that animals can express themselves in remunerative English, and no magazine goes to press nowadays without an animal story in it, except the old-style monthlies that are still running pictures of Bryan and the Mont Pelée horror.

But you needn't look for any stuck-up literature in my piece, such as Bearoo, the bear, and Snakoo, the snake, and Tammanoo, the tiger, talk in the jungle books. A yellow dog that's spent most of his life in a cheap New York flat sleeping in a corner on an old sateen underskirt (the one she spilled port wine on at the Lady 'Longshoremen's banquet), mustn't be expected to perform

O. HENRY

O. HENRY

any tricks with the art of speech.

I was born a yellow pup; date, locality, pedigree, and weight unknown. The first thing I can recollect, an old woman had me in a basket at Broadway and Twenty-third trying to sell me to a fat lady. Old Mother Hubbard was boosting me to beat the band as a genuine Pomeranian-Hambletonian-Red-Irish-Cochin-China-Stoke-Pogis fox terrier. The fat lady chased a V around among the samples of gros grain flannelette in her shopping bag till she cornered it, and gave up. From that moment I was a pet — a mamma's own wootsey squidlums. Say, gentle reader, did you ever have a 200-pound woman breathing a flavor of Camembert cheese and Peau d'Espagne pick you up and wallop her nose all over you, remarking all the time in an Emma Eames tone of voice: "Oh, oo's um oodlum, doodlum, woodlum, toodlum, bitsy-witsy skoodlums"?

From a pedigreed yellow pup I grew up to be an anonymous yellow cur looking like a cross between an Angora cat and a box of lemons. But my mistress never tumbled. She thought that the two primeval pups that Noah chased into the ark were but a collateral branch of my ancestors. It took two policemen to keep her from entering me at the Madison Square Garden for the Siberian bloodhound prize.

I'll tell you about that flat. The house was the ordinary thing in New York, paved with Parian marble in the entrance hall and cobblestones above the first floor. Our flat was three fl — well, not flights — climbs up. My mistress rented it unfurnished, and put in the regular things — 1903 antique upholstered parlor set, oil chromo of geishas in a Harlem tea house, rubber plant and husband.

By Sirius! there was a biped I felt sorry for. He was a little man with sandy hair and whiskers a good deal like mine. Henpecked? — well, toucans and flamingoes and pelicans all

had their bills in him. He wiped the dishes and listened to my mistress tell about the cheap, ragged things the lady with the squirrel-skin coat on the second floor hung out on her line to dry. And every evening while she was getting supper she made him take me out on the end of a string for a walk.

If men knew how women pass the time when they are alone they'd never marry. Laura Jean Libbey, peanut brittle, a little almond cream on the neck muscles, dishes unwashed, half an hour's talk with the iceman, reading a package of old letters, a couple of pickles and two bottles of malt extract, one hour peeking through a hole in the window shade into the flat across the air-shaft — that's about all there is to it. Twenty minutes before time for him to come home from work she straightens up the house, fixes her rat so it won't show, and gets out a lot of sewing for a ten-minute bluff.

I led a dog's life in that flat. 'Most all day I lay there in my corner watching that fat woman kill time. I slept sometimes and had pipe dreams about being out chasing cats into basements and growling at old ladies with black mittens, as a dog was intended to do. Then she would pounce upon me with a lot of that drivelling poodle palaver and kiss me on the nose — but what could I do? A dog can't chew cloves.

I began to feel sorry for Hubby, dog my cats if I didn't. We looked so much alike that people noticed it when we went out; so we shook the streets that Morgan's cab drives down, and took to climbing the piles of last December's snow on the streets where cheap people live.

One evening when we were thus promenading, and I was trying to look like a prize St. Bernard, and the old man was trying to look like he wouldn't have murdered the first organ-grinder he heard play Mendelssohn's wedding-march, I looked up at him and said, in my way:

"What are you looking so sour about, you oakum trimmed lobster? She don't kiss you.

You don't have to sit on her lap and listen to talk that would make the book of a musical comedy sound like the maxims of Epictetus. You ought to be thankful you're not a dog. Brace up, Benedick, and bid the blues begone."

The matrimonial mishap looked down at me with almost canine intelligence in his face.

"Why, doggie," says he, "good doggie. You almost look like you could speak. What is it, doggie — Cats?"

Cats! Could speak!

But, of course, he couldn't understand. Humans were denied the speech of animals. The only common ground of communication upon which dogs and men can get together is in fiction.

In the flat across the hall from us lived a lady with a black-and-tan terrier. Her husband strung it and took it out every evening, but he always came home cheerful and whistling. One day I touched noses with the black-and-tan in the hall, and I struck him for an elucidation.

"See here, Wiggle-and-Skip," I says, "you know that it ain't the nature of a real man to play dry nurse to a dog in public. I never saw one leashed to a bow-wow yet that didn't look like he'd like to lick every other man that looked at him. But your boss comes in every day as perky and set up as an amateur prestidigitator doing the egg trick. How does he do it? Don't tell me he likes it."

"Him?" says the black-and-tan. "Why, he uses Nature's Own Remedy. He gets spifflicated. At first when we go out he's as shy as the man on the steamer who would rather play pedro when they make 'em all jackpots. By the time we've been in eight saloons he don't care whether the thing on the end of his line is a dog or a catfish. I've lost two inches of my tail trying to sidestep those swinging doors."

21

O. HENRY

The pointer I got from that terrier — vaudeville please copy — set me to thinking.

One evening about 6 o'clock my mistress ordered him to get busy and do the ozone act for Lovey. I have concealed it until now, but that is what she called me. The black-and-tan was called "Tweetness." I consider that I have the bulge on him as far as you could chase a rabbit. Still "Lovey" is something of a nomenclatural tin can on the tail of one's self-respect.

At a quiet place on a safe street I tightened the line of my custodian in front of an attractive, refined saloon. I made a dead-ahead scramble for the doors, whining like a dog in the press despatches that lets the family know that little Alice is bogged while gathering lilies in the brook.

"Why, darn my eyes," says the old man, with a grin; "darn my eyes if the saffron-colored son of a seltzer lemonade ain't asking me in to take a drink. Lemme see — how long's it been since I saved shoe leather by keeping one foot on the foot-rest? I believe I'll —— "

I knew I had him. Hot Scotches he took, sitting at a table. For an hour he kept the Campbells coming. I sat by his side rapping for the waiter with my tail, and eating free lunch such as mamma in her flat never equalled with her homemade truck bought at a delicatessen store eight minutes before papa comes home.

When the products of Scotland were all exhausted except the rye bread the old man unwound me from the table leg and played me outside like a fisherman plays a salmon. Out there he took off my collar and threw it into the street.

"Poor doggie," says he; "good doggie. She shan't kiss you any more. 'Sa darned shame. Good doggie, go away and get run over by a street car and be happy."

I refused to leave. I leaped and frisked around the old man's legs happy as a pug on a rug.

"You old flea-headed woodchuck-chaser," I said to him — "you moon-baying, rabbit-

pointing, egg-stealing old beagle, can't you see that I don't want to leave you? Can't you see that we're both Pups in the Wood and the missis is the cruel uncle after you with the dish towel and me with the flea liniment and a pink bow tie to on my tail. Why not cut that all out and be pards forever more?"

Maybe you'll say he didn't understand — maybe he didn't. But he kind of got a grip on the Hot Scotches, and stood still for a minute, thinking.

"Doggie," says he, finally, "we don't live more than a dozen lives on this earth, and very few of us live to be more than 300. If I ever see that flat any more I'm a flat, and if you do you're flatter; and that's no flattery. I'm offering 60 to 1 that Westward Ho wins out by the length of a dachshund."

There was no string, but I frolicked along with my master to the Twenty-third Street ferry. And the cats on the route saw reason to give thanks that prehensile claws had been given them.

On the Jersey side my master said to a stranger who stood eating a currant bun:

"Me and my doggie, we are bound for the Rocky Mountains."

But what pleased me most was when my old man pulled both of my ears until I howled, and said:

"You common, monkey-headed, rat-tailed, sulphur-colored son of a door mat, do you know what I'm going to call you?"

I thought of "Lovey," and I whined dolefully.

"I'm going to call you 'Pete,' says my master; and if I'd had five tails I couldn't have done enough wagging to do justice to the occasion.

LASSIE COME HOME

The dog had met the boy by the school gate for five years. Now she couldn't understand that times were changed and she wasn't supposed to be there any more. But the boy knew.

So when he opened the door of the cottage, he spoke before he entered.

"Mother," he said, "Lassie's come home again."

He waited a moment, as if in hope of something. But the man and woman inside the cottage did not speak.

"Come in, Lassie," the boy said.

He held open the door, and the tricolor collie walked in obediently. Going head down, as a collie when it knows something is wrong, it went to the rug and lay down before the hearth, a black-white-and-gold

KNIGHT

25

aristocrat. The man, sitting on a low stool by the fireside, kept his eyes turned away. The woman went to the sink and busied herself there.

"She were waiting at school for me, just like always," the boy went on. He spoke fast, as if racing against time. "She must ha' got away again. I thought, happen this time, we might just — "

"No!" the woman exploded.

The boy's carelessness dropped. His voice rose in pleading.

"But this time, mother! Just this time. We could hide her. They wouldn't ever know."

"Dogs, dogs, dogs!" the woman cried. The words poured from her as if the boy's pleading had been a signal gun for her own anger. "I'm sick o' hearing about tykes round this house. Well, she's sold and gone and done with, so the quicker she's taken back the better. Now get her back quick, or first thing ye know we'll have Hynes round here again. Mr. Hynes!"

Her voice sharpened in imitation of the Cockney accent of the south: "Hi know you Yorkshiremen and yer come-'ome dogs. Training yer dogs to come 'ome so's yer can sell 'em hover and hover again.

"Well, she's sold, so ye can take her out o' my house and home to them as bought her!"

The boy's bottom lip crept out stubbornly, and there was silence in the cottage. Then the dog lifted its head and nudged the man's hand, as a dog will when asking for patting. But the man drew away and stared, silently, into the fire.

The boy tried again, with the ceaseless guile of a child, his voice coaxing.

"Look, feyther, she wants thee to bid her welcome. Aye, she's that glad to be home. Happen they don't tak' good care on her up there? Look, her coat's a bit poorly, don't ye think? A bit o' linseed strained through her drinking water — that's what I'd gi' her."

KNIGHT

Still looking in the fire, the man nodded. But the woman, as if perceiving the boy's new attack, sniffed.

"Aye, tha wouldn't be a Carraclough if tha didn't know more about tykes nor breaking eggs wi' a stick. Nor a Yorkshireman. My goodness, it seems to me sometimes that chaps in this village thinks more on their tykes nor they do o' their own flesh and blood. They'll sit by their firesides and let their own bairns starve so long as t' dog gets fed."

The man stirred, suddenly, but the boy cut in quickly.

"But she does look thin. Look, truly — they're not feeding her right. Just look!"

"Aye," the woman chattered. "I wouldn't put it past Hynes to steal t' best part o' t' dog meat for himself. And Lassie always was a strong eater."

"She's fair thin now," the boy said.

Almost unwillingly the man and woman looked at the dog for the first time.

"My gum, she is off a bit," the woman said. Then she caught herself. "Ma goodness, I suppose I'll have to fix her a bit o' summat. She can do wi' it. But soon as she's fed, back she goes. And never another dog I'll have in my house. Never another. Cooking and nursing for 'em, and as much trouble to bring up as a bairn!"

So, grumbling and chatting as a village woman will, she moved about, warming a pan of food for the dog. The man and boy watched the collie eat. When it was done, the boy took from the mantelpiece a folded cloth and a brush, and began prettying the collie's coat. The man watched for several minutes, and then could stand it no longer.

"Here," he said.

He took the cloth and brush from the boy and began working expertly on the dog, rubbing the rich, deep coat, then brushing the snowy whiteness of the full ruff and the apron, bringing

KNIGHT

out the heavy leggings on the forelegs. He lost himself in his work, and the boy sat on the rug, watching contentedly. The woman stood it as long as she could.

"Now will ye please tak' that tyke out o' here?"

The man flared in anger.

"Well, ye wouldn't have me tak' her back looking like a mucky Monday wash, wouldta?"

He bent again, and began fluffing out the collie's petticoats.

"Joe!" the woman pleaded. "Will ye tak' her out o' here? Hynes'll be nosing round afore ye know it. And I won't have that man in my house. Wearing his hat inside, and going on like he's the duke himself — him and his leggings!"

"All right, lass."

"And this time, Joe, tak' young Joe wi' ye."

"What for?"

"Well, let's get the business done and over with. It's him that Lassie runs away for. She comes for young Joe. So if he went wi' thee, and told her to stay, happen she'd be content and not run away no more, and then we'd have a little peace and quiet in the home — though heaven knows there's not much hope o' that these days, things being like they are." The woman's voice trailed away, as if she would soon cry in weariness.

The man rose. "Come, Joe," he said. "Get thy cap."

The Duke of Rudling walked along the gravel paths of his place with his granddaughter, Philippa. Philippa was a bright and knowing young woman, allegedly the only member of the duke's family he could address in unspotted language. For it was also alleged that the duke was the most irascible, vile-tempered old man in the three Ridings of Yorkshire.

29

KNIGHT

"Country going to pot!" the duke roared, stabbing at the walk with his great blackthorn stick. "When I was a young man! Hah! Women today not as pretty. Horses today not as fast. As for dogs — ye don't see dogs today like — "

Just then the duke and Philippa came round a clump of rhododendrons and saw a man, a boy and a dog.

"Ah," said the duke, in admiration. Then his brow knotted. "Damme, Carraclough! What're ye doing with my dog?"

He shouted it quite as if the others were in the next county, for it was also the opinion of the Duke of Rudling that people were not nearly so keen of hearing as they used to be when he was a young man.

"It's Lassie," Carraclough said. "She runned away again and I brought her back."

Carraclough lifted his cap, and poked the boy to do the same, not in any servile gesture, but to show that they were as well brought up as the next.

"Damme, ran away again!" the duke roared. "And I told that utter nincompoop Hynes to — where is he? Hynes! Hynes! Damme, Hynes, what're ye hiding for?"

"Coming, your lordship!" sounded a voice, far away behind the shrubberies. And soon Hynes appeared, a sharp-faced man in check coat, riding breeches, and the cloth leggings that grooms wear.

"Take this dog," roared the duke, "and pen her up! And damme, if she breaks out again, I'll — I'll — "

The duke waved his great stick threateningly, and then, without so much as a thank you or kiss the back of my hand to Joe Carraclough, he went stamping and muttering away.

"I'll pen 'er up," Hynes muttered, when the duke was gone. "And if she ever gets awye

agyne, I'll — "

He made as if to grab the dog, but Joe Carraclough's hob-nailed boot trod heavily on Hynes' foot.

"I brought my lad wi' me to bid her stay, so we'll pen her up this time. Eigh — sorry! I didn't see I were on thy foot. Come, Joe, lad."

They walked down the crunching gravel path, along by the neat kennel buildings. When Lassie was behind the closed door, she raced into the high wire run where she could see them as they went. She pressed close against the wire, waiting.

The boy stood close, too, his fingers through the meshes touching the dog's nose.

"Go on, lad," his father ordered. "Bid her stay!"

The boy looked around, as if for help that he did not find. He swallowed, and then spoke, low and quickly.

"Stay here, Lassie, and don't come home no more," he said. "And don't come to school for me no more. Because I don't want to see ye no more. 'Cause tha's a bad dog, and we don't love thee no more, and we don't want thee. So stay there forever and leave us be, and don't never come home no more."

Then he turned, and because it was hard to see the path plainly, he stumbled. But his father, who was holding his head very high as they walked away from Hynes, shook him savagely, and snapped roughly: "Look where tha's going!"

Then the boy trotted beside his father. He was thinking that he'd never be able to understand why grownups sometimes were so bad-tempered with you, just when you needed them most.

KNIGHT

After that, there were days and days that passed, and the dog did not come to the school gate any more. So then it was not like old times. There were so many things that were not like old times.

The boy was thinking that as he came wearily up the path and opened the cottage door and heard his father's voice, tense with anger: ". . . walk my feet off. If tha thinks I like — "

Then they heard his opening of the door and the voice stopped and the cottage was silent.

That's how it was now, the boy thought. They stopped talking in front of you. And this, somehow, was too much for him to bear.

He closed the door, ran out into the night, and onto the moor, that great flat expanse of land where all the people of that village walked in lonesomeness when life and its troubles seemed past bearing.

A long while later, his father's voice cut through the darkness.

"What's tha doing out here, Joe lad?"

"Walking."

"Aye."

They went on together, aimlessly, each following his own thoughts. And they both thought about the dog that had been sold.

"Tha maun't think we're hard on thee, Joe," the man said at last. "It's just that a chap's got to be honest. There's that to it. Sometimes, when a chap doesn't have much, he clings right hard to what he's got. And honest is honest, and there's no two ways about it.

"Why, look, Joe. Seventeen year I worked in that Clarabelle Pit till she shut down, and a good collier too. Seventeen year! And butties I've had by the dozen, and never a man of 'em can ever say that Joe Carraclough kept what wasn't his, nor spoke what wasn't true. Not a

33

KNIGHT

man in his Riding can ever call a Carraclough mishonest.

"And when ye've sold a man summat, and ye've taken his brass, and ye've spent it — well, then done's done. That's all. And ye've got to stand by that."

"But Lassie was — "

"Now, Joe! Ye can't alter it, ever. It's done — and happen it's for t' best. No two ways, Joe, she were getting hard to feed. Why, ye wouldn't want Lassie to be going around getting peaked and pined, like some chaps round here keep their tykes. And if ye're fond of her, then just think on it that now she's got lots to eat, and a private kennel, and a good run to herself, and living like a varritable princess, she is. Ain't that best for her?"

"We wouldn't pine her. We've always got lots to eat."

The man blew out his breath, angrily. "Eigh, Joe, nowt pleases thee. Well then, tha might as well have it. Tha'll never see Lassie no more. She run home once too often, so the duke's taken her wi' him up to his place in Scotland, and there she'll stay. So it's good-by and good luck to her, and she'll never come home no more, she won't. Now, I weren't off to tell thee, but there it is, so put it in thy pipe and smoke it, and let's never say a word about it no more — especially in front of thy mother."

The boy stumbled on in the darkness. Then the man halted.

"We ought to be getting back, lad. We left thy mother alone."

He turned the boy about, and then went on, but as if he were talking to himself.

"Tha sees, Joe, women's not like men. They have to stay home and manage best they can, and just spend the time in wishing. And when things don't go right, well, they have to take it out in talk and give a man hell. But it don't mean nowt, really, so tha shouldn't mind when thy mother talks hard.

KNIGHT

"Ye just got to learn to be patient and let 'em talk, and just let it go up t' chimney wi' th' smoke."

Then they were quiet, until, over the rise, they saw the lights of the village. Then the boy spoke: "How far away is Scotland, feyther?"

"Nay, lad, it's a long, long road."

"But how far, feyther?"

"I don't know — but it's a longer road than thee or me'll ever walk. Now, lad. Don't fret no more, and try to be a man — and don't plague thy mother no more, wilta?"

Joe Carraclough was right. It is a long road, as they say in the North, from Yorkshire to Scotland. Much too far for a man to walk — or a boy. And though the boy often thought of it, he remembered his father's words on the moor, and he put the thought behind him.

But there is another way of looking at it; and that's the distance from Scotland to Yorkshire. And that is just as far as from Yorkshire to Scotland. A matter of about four hundred miles, it would be, from the Duke of Rudling's place far up in the Highlands, to the village of Holdersby. That would be for a man, who could go fairly straight.

To an animal, how much farther would it be? For a dog can study no maps, read no signposts, ask no directions. It could only go blindly, by instinct, knowing that it must keep on to the south, to the south. It would wander and err, quest and quarter, run into firths and lochs that would send it side-tracking and back-tracking before it could go again on its way — south.

A thousand miles, it would be, going that way — a thousand miles over strange terrain.

There would be moors to cross, and burns to swim. And then those great, long lochs that

KNIGHT

stretch almost from one side of that dour land to another would bar the way and send a dog questing a hundred miles before it could find a crossing that would allow it to go south.

And, too, there would be rivers to cross, wide rivers like the Forth and the Clyde, the Tweed and the Tyne, where one must go miles to find bridges. And the bridges would be in towns. And in the towns there would be officials — like the one in Lanarkshire. In all his life he had never let a captured dog get away — except one. That one was a gaunt, snarling collie that whirled on him right in the pound itself, and fought and twisted loose to race away down the city street — going south.

But there are also kind people, too; ones knowing and understanding in the ways of dogs. There was an old couple in Durham who found a dog lying exhausted in a ditch one night — lying there with its head to the south. They took that dog into their cottage and warmed it and fed it and nursed it. And because it seemed an understanding, wise dog, they kept it in their home, hoping it would learn to be content. But, as it grew stronger, every afternoon toward four o'clock it would go to the door and whine, and then begin pacing back and forth between the door and the window, back and forth as the animals do in their cages at the zoo.

They tried every wile and every kindness to make it bide with them, but finally, when the dog began to refuse food, the old people knew what they must do. Because they understood dogs, they opened the door one afternoon and they watched a collie go, not down the road to the right, or to the left, but straight across a field toward the south; going steadily at a trot, as if she knew it still had a long, long road to travel.

Ah, a thousand miles of tor and brae, of shire and moor, of path and road and plowland, of river and stream and burn and brook and beck, of snow and rain and fog and sun, is a long way, even for a human being. But it would seem too far — much, much too far — for

KNIGHT

any dog to travel blindly and win through.

And yet — and yet — who shall say why, when so many weeks had passed that hope against hope was dying, a boy coming out of school, out of the cloakroom that always smelled of damp wool drying, across the concrete play yard with the black, waxed slides, should turn his eyes to a spot by the school gate from force of five years of habit, and see there a dog? Not a dog, this one, that lifted glad ears above a proud, slim head with its black-and-gold mask; but a dog that lay weakly, trying to lift a head that would no longer lift, trying to wag a tail that was torn and blotched and matted with dirt and burs, and managing to do nothing much except to whine in a weak, happy, crying way as a boy on his knees threw arms about it, and hands touched it that had not touched it for many a day.

Then who shall picture the urgency of a boy, running, awkwardly, with a great dog in his arms running through the village, past the empty mill, past the Labor Exchange, where the men looked up from their deep ponderings on life and the dole? Or who shall describe the high tones of a voice — a boy's voice, calling as he runs up a path: "Mother! Oh, mother! Lassie's come home! Lassie's come home!"

Nor does anyone who ever owned a dog need to be told the sound a man makes as he bends over a dog that has been his for many years; nor how a woman moves quickly, preparing food — which might be the family's condensed milk stirred into warm water; nor how the jowl of a dog is lifted so that raw egg and brandy, bought with precious pence, should be spooned in; nor how bleeding pads are bandaged, tenderly.

That was one day. There was another day when the woman in the cottage sighed with pleasure, for a dog lifted itself to its feet for the first time to stand over a bowl of oatmeal, putting its head down and lapping again and again while its pinched flanks quivered.

KNIGHT

And there was another day when the boy realized that, even now, the dog was not to be his again. So the cottage rang again with protests and cries, and a woman shrilling: "Is there never to be no more peace in my house and home?" Long after he was in bed that night the boy heard the rise and fall of the woman's voice, and the steady, reiterative tone of the man's. It went on long after he was asleep.

In the morning the man spoke, not looking at the boy, saying the words as if he had long rehearsed them.

"Thy mother and me have decided upon it that Lassie shall stay here till she's better. Anyhow, nobody could nurse her better than us. But the day that t' duke comes back, then back she goes, too. For she belongs to him, and that's honest, too. Now tha has her for a while, so be content."

In childhood, "for a while" is such a great stretch of days when seen from one end. It is a terribly short time seen from the other.

The boy knew how short it was that morning as he went to school and saw a motorcar driven by a young woman. And in the car was a gray-thatched, terrible old man, who waved a cane and shouted: "Hi! Hi, there! Damme, lad! You there! Hi!"

Then it was no use running, for the car could go faster than you, and soon it was beside you and the man was saying: "Damme, Philippa, will you make this smelly thing stand still a moment? Hi, lad!"

"Yes, sir."

"You're What's-'is-Name's lad, aren't you?"

"Ma feyther's Joe Carraclough."

"I know. I know. Is he home now?"

KNIGHT

"No, sir. He's away to Allerby. A mate spoke for him at the pit and he's gone to see if there's a chance."

"When'll he be back?"

"I don't know. I think about tea."

"Eh, yes. Well, yes. I'll drop round about fivish to see that father of yours. Something important."

It was hard to pretend to listen to lessons. There was only waiting for noon. Then the boy ran home.

"Mother! T' duke is back and he's coming to take Lassie away."

"Eigh, drat my buttons. Never no peace in this house. Is tha sure?"

"Aye. He stopped me. He said tell feyther he'll be round at five. Can't we hide her? Oh, mother."

"Nay, thy feyther — "

"Won't you beg him? Please, please. Beg feyther to — "

"Young Joe, now it's no use. So stop thy teasing! Thy feyther'll not lie. That much I'll give him. Come good, come bad, he'll not lie."

"But just this once, mother. Please beg him, just this once. Just one lie wouldn't hurt him. I'll make it up to him. I will. When I'm growed up, I'll get a job. I'll make money. I'll buy him things — and you, too. I'll buy you both anything you want if you'll only — "

For the first time in his trouble the boy became a child, and the mother, looking over, saw the tears that ran openly down his contorted face. She turned her face to the fire, and there was a pause. Then she spoke.

"Joe, tha mustn't," she said softly. "Tha must learn never to want nothing in life like that. It

41

don't do, lad. Tha mustn't want things bad, like tha wants Lassie."

The boy shook his clenched fists in impatience.

"It ain't that, mother. Ye don't understand. Don't ye see — it ain't me that wants her. It's her that wants us! Tha's wha made her come all them miles. It's her that wants us, so terrible bad!"

The woman turned and stared. It was as if, in that moment, she were seeing this child, this boy, this son of her own, for the first time in many years. She turned her head down toward the table. It was surrender.

"Come and eat, then," she said. "I'll talk to him. I will that, all right. I feel sure he won't lie. But I'll talk to him, all right. I'll talk to Mr. Joe Carraclough. I will indeed."

At five that afternoon, the Duke of Rudling, fuming and muttering, got out of a car at a cottage gate to find a boy barring his way. This was a boy who stood, stubbornly, saying fiercely: "Away wi' thee! Thy tyke's net here!"

"Damme, Philippa, th' lad's touched," the duke said. "He is. He's touched."

Scowling and thumping his stick, the old duke advanced until the boy gave way, backing down the path out of the reach of the waving blackthorn stick.

"Thy tyke's net here," the boy protested.

"What's he saying?" the girl asked.

"Says my dog isn't here. Damme, you going deaf? I'm supposed to be deaf, and I hear him plainly enough. Now, ma lad, what tyke o' mine's net here?"

As he turned to the boy, the duke spoke in broadest Yorkshire, as he did always to the people of the cottages — a habit which the Duchess of Rudling, and many more members

of the duke's family, deplored.

"Coom, coom, ma lad. Whet tyke's net here?"

"No tyke o' thine. Us hasn't got it." The words began running faster and faster as the boy backed away from the fearful old man who advanced. "No tyke could have done it. No tyke can come all them miles. It isn't Lassie. It's another one that looks like her. It isn't Lassie!"

"Why, bless ma heart and sowl," the duke puffed. "Where's thy father, ma lad?"

The door behind the boy opened, and a woman's voice spoke.

"If it's Joe Carraclough ye want, he's out in the shed — and been there shut up half the afternoon."

"What's this lad talking about — a dog of mine being here?"

"Nay," the woman snapped quickly. "He didn't say a tyke o' thine was here. He said it wasn't here."

"Well, what dog o' mine isn't here, then?"

The woman swallowed, and looked about as if for help. The duke stood, peering from under his jutting eyebrows. Her answer, truth or lie, was never spoken, for then they heard the rattle of a door opening, and a man making a pursing sound with his lips, as he will when he wants a dog to follow, and then Joe Carraclough's voice said: "This is t' only tyke us has here. Does it look like any dog that belongs to thee?"

With his mouth opening to cry one last protest, the boy turned. And his mouth stayed open. For there he saw his father, Joe Carraclough, the collie fancier, standing with a dog at his heels — a dog that sat at his left heel patiently, as any well-trained dog should do — as Lassie used to do. But this dog was not Lassie. In fact, it was ridiculous to think of it at the same moment as you thought of Lassie.

KNIGHT

For where Lassie's skull was aristocratic and slim, this dog's head was clumsy and rough. Where Lassie's ears stood in twin-lapped symmetry, this dog had one ear draggling and the other standing up Alsatian fashion in a way to give any collie breeder the cold shivers. Where Lassie's coat was a rich tawny gold, this dog's coat had ugly patches of black; and where Lassie's apron was a billowing stretch of snow-white, this dog had puddles of off-color blue-merle mixture. Besides, Lassie had four white paws, and this one had one paw white, two dirty-brown, and one almost black.

That is the dog they all looked at as Joe Carraclough stood there, having told no lie, having only asked a question. They all stood, waiting the duke's verdict.

But the duke said nothing. He only walked forward, slowly, as if he were seeing a dream. He bent beside the collie, looking with eyes that were as knowing about dogs as any Yorkshireman alive. And those eyes did not waste themselves upon twisted ears, or blotched marking, or rough head. Instead they were looking at a paw that the duke lifted, looking at the underside of the paw, staring intently at five black pads, crossed and recrossed with the scars where thorns had lacerated, and stones had torn.

For a long time the duke stared, and when he got up he did not speak in Yorkshire accents any more. He spoke as a gentleman should, and he said: "Joe Carraclough. I never owned this dog. 'Pon my soul, she's never belonged to me. Never!"

Then he turned and went stumping down the path, thumping his cane and saying: "Bless my soul. Four hundred miles! Damme, wouldn't ha' believed it. Damme — five hundred miles!"

He was at the gate when his granddaughter whispered to him fiercely.

"Of course," he cried. "Mind your own business. Exactly what I came for. Talking about

dogs made me forget. Carraclough! Carraclough! What're ye hiding for?"

"I'm still here, sir."

"Ah, there you are. You working?"

"Eigh, now. Working," Joe said. That's the best he could manage.

"Yes, working, working!" The duke fumed.

"Well, now — " Joe began.

Then Mrs. Carraclough came to his rescue, as a good housewife in Yorkshire will.

"Why, Joe's got three or four things that he's been considering," she said, with proper display of pride. "But he hasn't quite said yes or no to any of them yet."

"Then say no, quick," the old man puffed. "Had to sack Hynes. Didn't know a dog from a drunken filly. Should ha' known all along no damn Londoner could handle dogs fit for Yorkshire taste. How much, Carraclough?"

"Seven pounds a week, and worth every penny," Mrs. Carraclough chipped in. "One o' them other offers may come up to eight," she lied, expertly. For there's always a certain amount of lying to be done in life, and when a woman's married to a man who has made a lifelong cult of being honest, then she's got to learn to do the lying for two.

"Five," roared the duke — who, after all, was a Yorkshireman, and couldn't help being a bit sharp about things that pertained to money.

"Six," said Mrs. Carraclough.

"Five pound ten," bargained the duke, cannily.

"Done," said Mrs. Carraclough, who would have been willing to settle for three pounds in the first place. "But, o' course, us gets the cottage too."

"All right," puffed the duke. "Five pounds ten and the cottage. Begin Monday. But — on

KNIGHT

one condition. Carraclough, you can live on my land, but I won't have that thick-sculled, screw-lugged, gay-tailed eyesore of a misshapen mongrel on my property. Now never let me see her again. You'll get rid of her?"

He waited, and Joe fumbled for words. But it was the boy who answered, happily, gaily: "Oh, no, sir. She'll be waiting at school for me most o' the time. And, anyway, in a day or so we'll have her fixed up and coped up so's ye'd never, never recognize her."

"I don't doubt that," puffed the duke, as he went to the car. "I don't doubt ye could do just exactly that."

It was a long time afterward, in the car, that the girl said: "Don't sit there like a lion on the Nelson column. And I thought you were supposed to be a hard man."

"Fiddlesticks, m'dear. I'm a ruthless realist. For five years I've sworn I'd have that dog by hook or crook, and now, egad, at last I've got her."

"Pooh! You had to buy the man before you could get his dog."

"Well, perhaps that's not the worst part of the bargain."

DOGS

Every little wile you hear people talking about a man they don't nobody seem to have much use for him on acct. of him not paying his debts or beating his wife or something, and everybody takes a rap at him about this and that until finely one of the party speaks up and says theys must be some good in him because he likes animals.

"A man can't be all bad when he is so kind to dogs." That is what they generally always say and that is the reason you see so many men stop on the st. when they see a dog and pet it because they figure that maybe somebody will be looking at him do it, and the next time they are getting panned, why who ever seen it will speak up and say: "He can't be all bad because he likes dogs."

Well, friends, when you come right down

LARDNER

to cases they's about as much sence to this as a good many other delusions that we get here in this country, like for inst. the one about nobody wanting to win the first pot and the one about the whole lot of authors not being able to do their best work unless they are 1/2 pickled.

But if liking animals ain't a virtue in itself I don't see how it proves that a man has got any virtues, and personly, if I had a daughter and she wanted to get married and I asked her what kind of a bird the guy was and she said she don't know nothing about him except that one day she seen him kiss a leopard, why I would hold up my blessing till a few of the missing precincts was heard from.

But as long as our best people has got it in their skull that a friendly feeling toward dumb brutes takes the curse off a bad egg, why I or nobody else is going to be sucker enough to come out and admit that all the horses, rams and oxens in the world could drop dead tomorrow morning without us batting an eye.

Pretty near everybody wants to be well thought of and if liking dogs or sheep is a helping along these lines, why even if I don't like them, I wouldn't never lose a opportunity to be seen in their company and act as if I was having the time of my life.

But while I was raised in a Kennel, you might say, and some of my most intimate childhood friends was of the canine gender, still in all I believe dogs is better in some climates than others, the same as oysters, and I don't think it should ought to be held against a man if he don't feel the same towards N.Y. dogs as he felt towards Michigan dogs, and I am free to confess that the 4 dogs who I have grew to know personly here on Long Island have failed to arouse tender yearnings anyways near similar to those inspired by the flea bearers of my youth.

And in case they should be any tendency on the part of my readers to denounce me for

failing to respond whole heartedly to the wiles of the Long Island breed let me present a brief sketch of some so as true lovers of the canine tribe can judge for themselfs if the fault is all mind.

No. 1.

This was the dainty boy that belonged to Gene Buck and it was a bull dog no bigger than a 2 car garage and it wouldn't harm a hair of nobody's head only other animals and people. Children were as safe with this pet as walking in the Pittsburgh freight yards and he wouldn't think no more of wronging a cat than scratching himself.

In fairness to Mr. Buck I'll state that a pal of his give him the dog as a present without no comment. Well they wasn't no trouble till Gene had the dog pretty near 1/2 hour when they let him out. He was gone 10 minutes during which Gene received a couple of phone calls announcing more in anger than sorrow the sudden death of 2 adjacent cats of noble berth so when the dog came back Gene spanked him and give him a terrible scolding and after that he didn't kill no more cats except when he got outdoors.

But the next day De Wolf Hopper come over to call and brought his kid which the dog thought would look better with one leg and it took 5 people to get him not to operate, so after that Gene called up the Supt. of a dogs reform school and the man said he would take him and cure him of the cat habit by tying one of his victims around his neck and leaving it there for a week but he don't know how to cure the taste for young Hoppers unless De Wolf could spare the kid for a wk. after they was finished with the cat.

This proposition fell through but anyway Gene sent the dog to the reformatory and is still paying board for same.

LARDNER

No. 2.

The people that lived three houses from the undersigned decided to move to England where it seems like you can't take dogs no more, as they asked us did we want the dog and it was very nice around children and we took it and sure enough it was O.K. in regards to children but it shared this new owners feelings toward motorcycles and every time one went past the house the dog would run out and spill the contents and on Sundays when the traffic was heavy they would sometimes be as many as 4 or 5 motorcycles jehus standing on their heads in the middle of the road.

One of them finely took offense and told on the dog and the justice of the peace called me up and said I would have to kill it within 24 hrs. and the only way I could think of to do the same was drown it in the bath tub and if you done that, why the bath tub wouldn't be no good no more, because it was a good sized dog and no matter how often you pulled the stopper it would still be there.

No. 3.

The next door neighbors has a pro-German police dog that win a blue ribbon once but now it acts as body guard for the lady of the house and one day we was over there and the host says to slap his Mrs. on the arm and see what happened so I slapped her on the arm and I can still show you what happened.

When you dance with mine hostess this sweet little pet dances along with you and watches your step and if you tred on the lady's toes he fines you a mouthfull and if you and her is partners in a bridge game he lays under the table and you either bid right and play right or you get nipped.

LARDNER

No. 4.

This is our present incumbrance which we didn't ask for him and nobody give him to us but here he is and he has got insomnia and he has picked a spot outside my window to enjoy it but not only that but he has learnt that if you jump at a screen often enough it will finely give way and the result is that they ain't a door or window on the first floor that you couldn't drive a rhinoceros through it and all the bugs that didn't already live in the house is moving in and bringing their family.

That is a true record of the dogs who I have met since taking up my abode in Nassau County so when people ask me do I like dogs I say I'm crazy about them and I think they are all right in their place but it ain't Long Island.

BEING A PUBLIC
CHARACTER

Ever since I bit a circus lion, believing him to be another dog, only larger, I've been what Doc Watson calls a Public Character in our town.

Freckles, my boy, was a kind of Public Character, too. All the other boys and dogs in town sort of looked up to him and thought how lucky he was to belong to a dog like me. And he deserved all the glory he got out of it. For if I do say it myself, there's not a dog in town got a better boy than my boy Freckles. I'll back him against any dog's boy anywhere near his size for fighting, swimming, climbing, foot-racing or throwing stones farthest and straightest. Or I'll back him against any stray boy, either.

Well, some dogs may be born Public Characters and like it. And some may be brought up to like it. But with me, becoming

MARQUIS

a Public Character happened all in a flash, and it was sort of hard for me to get used to it. One day I was just a private sort of dog. And the next day I had bit that lion and fame came so sudden I scarcely knew how to act.

Even Heinie Hassenyager, the butcher got stuck on me after I got to be a Public Character. Heinie would come two blocks up Main Street with lumps of Hamburg steak, which is some kind one has already chewed for you, and give them to me. Steak, mind you, not old gristly scraps. And before I became a Public Character Heinie even begrudged me the bones I would drag out of the box under his counter when he wasn't looking.

My daily hope was that I could live up to it all. I had always tried, before I happened to bite that lion, to be a friendly kind of dog towards boys and humans and dogs, all three. I'd always been expected to do a certain amount of tail-wagging and be friendly. But as soon as I got to be a Public Character, I saw right away that I wasn't expected to be *too* friendly any more.

So when Heinie would bring me the ready-chewed steak I'd growl at him a little bit. And then I'd bolt and gobble the steak like I didn't think so darned much of it and was doing Heinie a big favor to eat it. That way of acting made a big hit with Heinie, too. I could see that he was honored and flattered because I didn't go any further than just a growl. And the more I growled, the more steak he brought. Everybody in town fed me. I pretty near ate myself to death for awhile, besides all the meat I buried back of Doc Watson's store to dig up later.

The worst of it was that people, after a week or so, began to expect me to pull something else remarkable. Freckles, he got up a circus, and charged pins and marbles, and cents, when he found anyone that had any, to get into it, and I was the principal part of that circus. I was in a cage. I didn't care for being caged and circused that way myself. And it was right at that circus that considerable trouble started.

MARQUIS

Seeing me in a cage like that, all famoused-up, with more meat poked through the slats than two dogs could eat, made Mutt Mulligan and some of my old friends jealous. Mutt, he nosed by the cage and sniffed. I nosed a piece of meat out of the cage to him. Mutt grabbed it and gobbled it down, but he didn't thank me any. Mutt, he says:

"There's a new dog down town that says he blew in from Chicago. He says he used to be a Blind Man's Dog on a street corner there. He's a pretty wise dog, and he's a right ornery-looking dog, too. He's peeled considerably where he has been bit in fights.

"You got such a swell head on you the last week or so that you gotta be licked. You can fool boys and humans all you want to about that accidental old lion, but us dogs got your number all right. What that Blind Man's Dog from Chicago would do to you would be a plenty!"

"Well then," I says, "I'll be out of this cage about supper time. Suppose you bring that Blind Man's Dog around here. And if he ain't got a spiked collar on him, I'll fight him. I won't fight a spiked-collared dog to please anybody."

And I wouldn't neither, without I had one on myself. If you can't get a dog by the throat or the back of his neck, what's the use of fighting him? You might just as well try to eat a black-smith shop as fight one of those spike-collared dogs.

Well, that night after supper, along comes the Blind Man's Dog. Never did I see a Blind Man's Dog that was as tight-skinned. I had been used to fighting loose-skinned dogs that you can get some sort of a reasonable hold on while you are working around for position. And running into a tight-skinned dog that way, all of a sudden and all unprepared for it, would make anybody nervous.

58

Lots of dogs wouldn't have fought him at all when they realized how they had been fooled

MARQUIS

about him, and how tight-skinned he was. But I was a Public Character now, and I had to fight him. More than that, I ain't ready to say yet that that dog actually licked me. Freckles he hit him with a lump of soft coal, and he got all off me and run away before I could get my second wind. There's no telling what I would have done to that Blind Man's Dog, tight-skinned as he was, if he hadn't run away before I got my second wind.

Well, there's some mighty peculiar dogs in this world, let alone boys and humans. The word got around town, in spite of his running away before I got my second wind, that the Blind Man's Dog had actually licked me! Every time Freckles and me went down the street some one would say:

"Well, the dog that licked the lion got licked himself, did he?"

And if it was a lady said it, Freckles would spit on the sidewalk through the place where his front teeth are out and pass on politely as if he hadn't heard and say nothing. And if it was a man that said it Freckles would thumb his nose at him. And if it was a girl, he would rub a handful of sand into her hair. And if it was a boy anywhere near his size, there would be a fight. If it was too big a boy, Freckles would sling railroad iron at him.

I didn't care so awful much for myself, but I hated it for Freckles. For one Saturday afternoon when there wasn't any school, instead of going swimming with the other kids or playing baseball, or anything, he went and played with girls. He must have been pretty well downhearted and felt himself pretty much of an outcast, or he wouldn't have done that. I am an honest dog, and the truth must be told, the disgrace along with everything else, and the truth is that he played with girls of his own accord that day. Any boy will play with girls when all the boys and girls are playing together; but no boy is going to go off alone and look up a bunch of girls and play with them unless he has had considerable of a downfall.

MARQUIS

Right next to our side of the yard was the Wilkinses. Freckles was sitting on the top of their fence when the three Wilkins girls came out to play. There was only two boys in the Wilkins family, and they were twins; but they were only year-old babies and didn't amount to anything. The two oldest Wilkins girls each had one of the twins taking care of it. And the other Wilkins girl had one of those big dolls made as big as a baby. They were rolling those babies and the doll around the grass in a wheelbarrow, and the wheel came off, and that's how Freckles happened to go over.

"Up in the attic," says one, when he had fixed up the wheelbarrow, "there's a little old express wagon with one wheel off that would be better'n this wheelbarrow. Maybe you could fix that wheel on, too."

Freckles, he fell for it. After he got the wagon fixed, they got to playing charades and fool girl games like that. The hired girl was off for the afternoon, and pretty soon Mrs. Wilkins hollered up the stairs that she was going to be gone for an hour, and to take good care of the twins, and then we were alone in the place.

Well, it wasn't much fun for me. They played and they played and I stuck to Freckles. I stuck to him because a dog should stick to his boy, and a boy should stick to his dog, no matter what the disgrace. But after a while I got pretty tired and lay down on a rug, and a new kind of flea struck me. After I had chased him down and cracked him with my teeth I went to sleep.

I must have slept pretty sound and pretty long. All of a sudden I waked up with a start and almost choking, for the place was smoky. I barked and no one answered.

The house was on fire, and it looked like I was alone in it. I went down the back stairway but the door that led out on the first floor landing was locked and I had to go up again. By the time I got back up, the front stairway was a great deal fuller of smoke, and I could see glints of flame through it way down below. But it was the only way out of the place.

On the top step I stumbled over a gray wool bunch of something or other, and I picked it up in my mouth. Think I, "That's Freckle's gray sweater that he is so stuck on. I might as well take it down to him."

I got kind of confused and excited. And it struck me all of a sudden, by the time I was down to the second floor, that the sweater weighed an awful lot. I dropped it on the second floor, and ran into one of the front bedrooms and looked out.

The whole town was in the front yard and in the street. And in the midst of the crowd was Mrs. Wilkins, carrying on like mad. "My baby!" she yelled. "Save my baby. Let me loose! I'm going after my baby!"

I stood up on my hind legs, with my head just out of that bedroom window, and the flame and smoke licking up all around me, and barked. "My doggie! My doggie!" yells Freckles, who was in the crowd. And he made a run for the house, but someone grabbed him and slung him back.

And Mrs. Wilkins made a run, but they held her, too. Old Pop Wilkins, Mrs. Wilkins's husband, was jumping up and down in front of Mrs. Wilkins yelling, here was her baby. He had a real baby on one arm and that big doll in the other, and was so excited he thought he had both babies. Later I heard what had happened. The kids had thought that they were getting out with both twins but one of them had saved the doll and left a twin behind.

Well, I thinks that the baby will likely turn up in the crowd, and I'd better get out of there myself while the getting was good. I ran out of the bedroom, and run into that hunched-up gray bundle again.

MARQUIS

I ain't saying I knew it was the missing twin in a gray shawl when I picked it up a second time. And I ain't saying I didn't know it. The fact is I did pick it up. It may be that I was so rattled I just picked it up because I had had it in my mouth before and didn't quite know what I was doing. But the *record* is something you can't go behind, and the record is that I got out the back way and into the backyard with that bundle swinging from my mouth, and walked around into the front yard and laid that bundle down — *and it was the twin!*

I don't make any claim that I *knew* it was the twin till I got into the front yard. But you can't prove I *didn't* know it was. And nobody tried to prove it. The gray bundle let out a squall.

"My baby!" yells Mrs. Wilkins. And she kissed me.

"Three cheers for Spot!" yelled the whole town. And they give them.

And then I saw what the lay of the land was, so I wagged my tail and barked. It called for hero stuff, and I throwed my head up and looked noble — and pulled it.

An hour before Freckles and me had been outcasts. And now we was Public Characters again. We walked down Main Street and we owned it. And we hadn't any more got to Doc Watson's drug store than in rushed Heinie Hassenyager with a Hamburg steak, and with tears in his eyes.

"It's got chicken livers mixed in it, too!" says Heinie.

I ate it. But while I ate it, I growled at him.

TOWARD THE DOG DAYS

There will always, I suppose, be people who go about declaring that the city is no place for dogs. There will also always be, I expect, forest fires, wet rice pudding with raisins, influenza, motion-picture magazines, and fancy galoshes. You can't hope to get away from them, and it is best to abandon endeavor. They all come under the head of This Living.

Perhaps it is well to admit, either for the sake or the suppression of argument, that the city *is* no place for dogs. Then the matter can rest right there, and everything may go along as usual. Neither the city nor the pups will mind in the least. They will just keep right on getting along beautifully with one another.

Some of my best friends are city-dwelling

PARKER

dogs, and I have yet to hear a word of complaint from any one of them. True, they are not above making something of a spectacle of themselves when they get back to Mother Nature for an unleashed run in the grass, yet the general attitude seems to be that the country is all right for a visit, but they wouldn't live here if you gave them the place. And it is obvious that the city must offer an ambitious young dog far more opportunities than he could find on the farm, for more and more dogs are coming to New York every day. The streets are thronged with them. The outlands must be practically deserted.

I do believe that you should select for your personal use, if you live in the city, a dog whose size recommends him for metropolitan life. Anything larger than a Shetland pony is perhaps a shade impractical. It is true that the sights of the town include the three beautiful, exquisitely conditioned Great Danes who are daily led up Fifth Avenue for their walk in the park, and I know intimately an Irish deer-hound who has lived all his life in a studio apartment, is practically bubbling over with health and high spirits, and is the delight of his home circle. But these may be exceptions. A big dog may get on delightfully, himself, in town, yet the strain on the family life may prove too intense. There was that Airedale I had once, I remember. It was during his reign that my apartment came to be known, among my friends, as the Black Hole of Calcutta.

You see, when he came into my life, he was seven weeks old and about the size of a three-dollar Teddy bear. And an Airedale would appear to be an entirely suitable dog for city wear; you see thousands of them — and I mean thousands — walking carefree and unconcerned along the avenues, usually with very pretty ladies respectfully occupying the other end of their leashes. But this was a sort of super-Airedale. In the wholesome air and sunlight of Manhattan, he grew and he grew until many people advised my entering him in the horse show. We

PARKER

would go out for a little walk, he and I, and my feet would never be on the ground during the entire excursion. Indoors, he developed the habit of sofa-eating; he became, indeed, a veritable addict. Give that dog an ordinary sofa, such as your furniture dealer would be glad to let you have for a nominal sum, and he could make a whole meal off it. If you ran out of sofas, he would be philosophical about the matter — he was always delightfully good-humored — and make a light snack of a chintz-covered arm-chair. Once, I recall, he went a-gypsying and used a set of Dickens, the one with the Cruikshank illustrations, for a picnic lunch.

"Now don't you worry about me," he would say. "You know how I am about what I eat — pot luck suits me best. For goodness' sake, don't make company of me. Anything you've got in the house will do."

It was eventually decided — and maybe you think that tears weren't shed over that decision! — that he was not the dog for an apartment existence. Given a stretch of countryside — a prairie, say — where he could run off his energies, he might be saved from the furniture habit. So he was awarded to a friend in the country. There was a sad scene at our parting. I was the sad scene. He never gave so much as a backward look. But that is ever my story. My dearest wish would be to be one to whom dogs gave all their devotion; but they always cast me off like a withered violet when any one else comes in the room. It is their indifference, I suppose, that holds me.

The trifler in question is at present leading a model and contented life in a New Jersey village, where, I believe, he is thinking of running for postmaster.

But he is the only dog from whom I have been parted by other than an act of Providence. I have always lived in the city and I have never been without a dog for more than two weeks at a stretch; a fortnight, I find, is as long as I can possibly go on in a dogless condition. The

PARKER

present incumbent alleges to be a Scottish terrier (the Scots get pretty bitter when the breed is referred to as Aberdeen terriers), although it is a bit difficult to ascertain upon what she bases her claims. She is, many admit, somewhat on the general model of a Scottie, but on a clear day you can see a remarkably definite strain of cocker spaniel. But it does not matter. She has It.

Daisy, her name is — possibly on the assumption that she won't tell. It is not the name that I should have selected; she was named that when I got her, on which day she immediately took over the management of my life. But her name doesn't matter, either. She couldn't be annoyed to answer to it, no matter what it was. She is, on the whole, a genial dog. The only things she really hates are horses; so strong is her feeling that she has dedicated her career to barking at them. It is her plan thus to frighten them out of town, indeed to put such a scare into them that they will never return. She is not quite nine inches tall.

There are those who say that she is not extraordinarily bright, but they are not to be believed for a moment. Why, that dog is practically a Phi Beta Kappa! She can sit up and beg, and she can give her paw — I don't say she will, but she can. And when you ask her if she wants to go out, do you know what she does? (I have always hoped that maybe some day she would say "No," but it has never happened yet.) She goes and fetches her leash, that's what she does. But there — you shouldn't have let me get started talking about her. Next thing you know I'll be showing you snapshots.

Possibly she insists upon being called a Scottish terrier because, at the moment, Scottish terriers are high in fashion — it is queer, isn't it that there should be fashions in dogs? Scotties are a sane style; they are, so to say, serviceable and they give good wear. They have all the compactness of a small dog and all the valor of a big one. And they are so exceedingly sturdy that it is proverbial that the only thing fatal to them is being run over by an automobile — in

69

which case the car itself knows that it has been in a fight.

Now is the time to see the dogs of New York at their best; they come out, these sweet spring mornings, as thick as crocuses and as cocky as blue-jays. The gay, swift, city spring is their time. In the winter, they are a bit too preoccupied to respond to your admiration, as they are pulled along by mistresses hurrying through the thin, gray cold. And in the summer, their ranks are greatly reduced, for the better-connected ones — I just stopped myself in time, for I was about to say the "doggier ones," and then, oh, what would you have thought of me? — have gone to the country, hunting rabbits in Westchester or retrieving rubber balls at the Hamptons, lured there, doubtless, by the promise that they will not have to stay long, and the additional proviso that nobody will offer to give them the place.

LOUIS

"It would be jolly to spend Easter in Vienna this year," said Strudwarden, "and look up some of my old friends there. It's about the jolliest place I know of to be at for Easter — "

"I thought we had made up our minds to spend Easter at Brighton," interrupted Lena Strudwarden, with an air of aggrieved surprise.

"You mean that you had made up your mind that we should spend Easter there," said her husband; "we spent last Easter there, and Whitsuntide as well, and the year before that we were at Worthing, and Brighton again before that. I think it would be just as well to have a real change of scene while we are about it.

"The journey to Vienna would be very expensive," said Lena.

"You are not often concerned about

SAKI

71

SAKI

economy," said Strudwarden, "and in any case the trip to Vienna won't cost a bit more than the rather meaningless luncheon parties we usually give to quite meaningless acquaintances at Brighton. To escape from all that set would be a holiday in itself."

Strudwarden spoke feelingly; Lena Strudwarden maintained an equally feeling silence on that particular subject. The set that she gathered round her at Brighton and other South Coast resorts was composed of individuals who might be dull and meaningless in themselves, but who understood the art of flattering Mrs. Strudwarden. She had no intention of foregoing their society and their homage and flinging herself among unappreciative strangers in a foreign capital.

"You must go to Vienna alone if you are bent on going," she said; "I couldn't leave Louis behind, and a dog is always a fearful nuisance in a foreign hotel, besides all the fuss and separation of the quarantine restrictions when one comes back. Louis would die if he was parted from me for even a week. You don't know what that would mean to me."

Lena stooped down and kissed the nose of the diminutive brown Pomeranian that lay, snug and irresponsive, beneath a shawl on her lap.

"Look here," said Strudwarden, "this eternal Louis business is getting to be a ridiculous nuisance. Nothing can be done, no plans can be made, without some veto connected with that animal's whims or convenience being imposed. If you were a priest in attendance on some African fetish you couldn't set up a more elaborate code of restrictions. I believe you'd ask the Government to put off a General Election if you thought it would interfere with Louis's comfort in any way."

By way of answer to this tirade Mrs. Strudwarden stooped down again and kissed the irresponsive brown nose. It was the action of a woman with a beautifully meek nature, who would, however, send the whole world to the stake sooner than yield an inch where she knew herself to be in the right.

72

"It isn't as if you were in the least bit fond of animals," went on Strudwarden, with growing

irritation; "when we are down at Kerryfield you won't stir a step to take the house dogs out, even if they're dying for a run, and I don't think you've been in the stables twice in your life. You laugh at what you call the fuss that's being made over the extermination of plumage birds, and you are quite indignant with me if I interfere on behalf of an ill-treated, over-driven animal on the road. And yet you insist on every one's plans being made subservient to the convenience of that stupid little morsel of fur and selfishness."

"You are prejudiced against my little Louis," said Lena, with a world of tender regret in her voice.

"I've never had the chance of being anything else but prejudiced against him," said Strudwarden; "I know what a jolly responsive companion a doggie can be, but I've never been allowed to put a finger near Louis. You say he snaps at any one except you and your maid, and you snatched him away from old Lady Peterby the other day, when she wanted to pet him, for fear he would bury his teeth in her. All that I ever see of him is the tip of his unhealthy-looking little nose, peeping out from his basket or from your muff, and I occasionally hear his wheezy little bark when you take him for a walk up and down the corridor. You can't expect one to get extravagantly fond of a dog of that sort. One might as well work up an affection for the cuckoo in a cuckoo-clock."

"He loves me," said Lena, rising from the table, and bearing the shawl-swathed Louis in her arms. "He loves only me, and perhaps that is why I love him so much in return. I don't care what you say against him, I am not going to be separated from him. If you insist on going to Vienna you must go alone, as far as I am concerned. I think it would be much more sensible if you were to come to Brighton with Louis and me, but of course you must please yourself."

"You must get rid of that dog," said Strudwarden's sister when Lena had left the room; "it must be helped to some sudden and merciful end. Lena is merely making use of it as an instrument for getting her own way on dozens of occasions when she would otherwise be obliged to yield gracefully to your wishes or to the general convenience. I am convinced that she doesn't care a brass button about the animal itself. When her friends are buzzing round her at Brighton or anywhere else and the dog would be in the way, it has to spend whole days alone with the maid, but if you want Lena to go with you anywhere where she doesn't want to go instantly she trots out the excuse that she couldn't be separated from her dog. Have you ever come into a room unobserved and heard Lena talking to her beloved pet? I never have. I believe she only fusses over it when there's some one present to notice her."

"I don't mind admitting," said Strudwarden, "that I've dwelt more than once lately on the possibility of some fatal accident putting an end to Louis's existence. It's not very easy, though, to arrange a fatality for a creature that spends most of its time in a muff or asleep in a toy kennel. I don't think poison would be any good; it's obviously horribly over-fed, for I've seen Lena offer it dainties at table sometimes, but it never seems to eat them."

"Lena will be away at church on Wednesday morning," said Elsie Strudwarden reflectively; "she can't take Louis with her there, and she is going on to the Dellings for lunch. That will give you several hours in which to carry out your purpose. The maid will be flirting with the chauffeur most of the time, and, anyhow, I can manage to keep her out of the way on some pretext or other."

"That leaves the field clear," said Strudwarden, "but unfortunately my brain is equally a blank as far as any lethal project is concerned. The little beast is so monstrously inactive; I can't pretend that it leapt into the bath and drowned itself, or that it took on the butcher's mastiff in unequal combat and got chewed up. In what possible guise could death come to a confirmed basket-dweller? It would be too suspicious if we invented a Suffragette raid and pretended that they invaded Lena's boudoir and threw a brick at him. We should have to do a lot of other damage as well, which would be rather a nuisance, and the servants would think it odd that they had seen nothing of the invaders."

"I have an idea," said Elsie; "get a box with an air-tight lid, and bore a small hole in it, just

big enough to let in an india-rubber tube. Pop Louis, kennel and all, into the box, shut it down, and put the other end of the tube over the gas-bracket. There you have a perfect lethal chamber. You can stand the kennel at the open window afterwards, to get rid of the smell of the gas, and all that Lena will find when she comes home late in the afternoon will be a placidly defunct Louis."

"Novels have been written about women like you," said Strudwarden; "you have a perfectly criminal mind. Let's come and look for a box."

Two mornings later the conspirators stood gazing guiltily at a stout square box, connected with the gas-bracket by a length of india-rubber tubing.

"Not a sound," said Elsie; "he never stirred; it must have been quite painless. All the same I feel rather horrid now it's done."

"The ghastly part has to come," said Strudwarden, turning off the gas. "We'll lift the lid slowly, and let the gas out by degrees. Swing the door to and fro to send a draught through the room."

Some minutes later, when the fumes had rushed off, he stooped down and lifted out the little kennel with its grim burden. Elsie gave an exclamation of terror. Louis sat at the door of his dwelling, head erect and ears pricked, as coldly and defiantly inert as when they had put him into his execution chamber. Strudwarden dropped the kennel with a jerk, and stared for a long moment at the miracle-dog; then he went into a peal of chattering laughter.

It was certainly a wonderful imitation of a truculent-looking toy Pomeranian, and the apparatus that gave forth a wheezy bark when you pressed it had materially helped the imposition that Lena, and Lena's maid, had foisted on the household. For a woman who disliked animals, but liked getting her own way under a halo of unselfishness, Mrs. Strudwarden had managed rather well.

"Louis is dead," was the curt information that greeted Lena on her return from her luncheon party.

"Louis *dead!*" she exclaimed.

"Yes, he flew at the butcher-boy and bit him, and he bit me too, when I tried to get him off, so I had tò have him destroyed. You warned me that he snapped, but you didn't tell me that he was down-right dangerous. I shall have to pay the boy something heavy by way of compensation, so you will have to go without those buckles that you wanted to have for Easter; also I shall have to go to Vienna to consult Dr. Schroeder, who is a specialist on dogbites, and you will have to come too. I have sent what remains of Louis to Rowland Ward to be stuffed; that will be my Easter gift to you instead of the buckles. For Heaven's sake, Lena, weep, if you really feel it so much; anything would be better than standing there staring as if you thought I had lost my reason."

Lena Strudwarden did not weep, but her attempt at laughing was an unmistakable failure.

THE DOG THAT BIT PEOPLE

Probably no one man should have as many dogs in his life as I have had, but there was more pleasure than distress in them for me except in the case of an Airedale named Muggs. He gave me more trouble than all the other fifty four or five put together, although my moment of keenest embarrassment was the time a Scotch terrier named Jeannie, who had just had six puppies in the clothes closet of a fourth floor apartment in New York, had the unexpected seventh and last at the corner of Eleventh Street and Fifth Avenue during a walk she had insisted on taking. Then, too, there was the prize-winning French poodle, a great big black poodle — none of your little, untroublesome white miniatures — who got sick riding in the rumble seat of a car with me on her way to the Greenwich Dog

THURBER

Show. She had a red rubber bib tucked around her throat and, since a rain storm came up when we were half way through the Bronx, I had to hold over her a small green umbrella, really more of a parasol. The rain beat down fearfully and suddenly the driver of the car drove into a big garage, filled with mechanics. It happened so quickly that I forgot to put the umbrella down and I will always remember, with sickening distress, the look of incredulity mixed with hatred that came over the face of the particular hardened garage man that came over to see what we wanted, when he took a look at me and the poodle. All garage men, and people of that intolerant stripe, hate poodles with their curious hair cut, especially the pompons that you have got to leave on their hips if you expect the dogs to win a prize.

But the Airedale, as I have said, was the worst of all my dogs. He really wasn't my dog, as a matter of fact: I came home from a vacation one summer to find that my brother Roy had bought him while I was away. A big, burly, choleric dog, he always acted as if he thought I wasn't one of the family. There was a slight advantage in being one of the family, for he didn't bite the family as often as he bit strangers. Still, in the years that we had him he bit everybody but mother, and he made a pass at her once but missed. That was during the month when we suddenly had mice, and Muggs refused to do anything about them. Nobody ever had mice exactly like the mice we had that month. They acted like pet mice, almost like mice somebody had trained. They were so friendly that one night when mother entertained at dinner the Friraliras, a club she and my father had belonged to for twenty years, she put down a lot of little dishes with food in them on the pantry floor so that the mice would be satisfied with that and wouldn't come into the dining room. Muggs stayed out in the pantry with the mice, lying on the floor, growling to himself — not at the mice, but about all the people in the next room that he would have liked to get at. Mother slipped out into the pantry once to see

how everything was going. Everything was going fine. It made her so mad to see Muggs lying there, oblivious of the mice — they came running up to her — that she slapped him and he slashed at her, but didn't make it. He was sorry immediately, mother said. He was always sorry, she said, after he bit someone, but we could not understand how she figured this out. He didn't act sorry.

Mother used to send a box of candy every Christmas to the people the Airedale bit. The list finally contained forty or more names. Nobody could understand why we didn't get rid of the dog. I didn't understand it very well myself, but we didn't get rid of him. I think that one or two people tried to poison Muggs — he acted poisoned once in a while — and old Major Moberly fired at him once with his service revolver near the Seneca Hotel in East Broad Street — but Muggs lived to be almost eleven years old and even when he could hardly get around he bit a Congressman who had called to see my father on business. My mother had never liked the Congressman — she said the signs of his horoscope showed he couldn't be trusted (he was Saturn with the moon in Virgo) — but she sent him a box of candy that Christmas. He sent it right back, probably because he suspected it was trick candy. Mother persuaded herself it was all for the best that the dog had bitten him, even though father lost an important business association because of it. "I wouldn't be associated with such a man," mother said. "Muggs could read him like a book."

We used to take turns feeding Muggs to be on his good side, but that didn't always work. He was never in a very good humor, even after a meal. Nobody knew exactly what was the matter with him, but whatever it was it made him irascible, especially in the mornings. Roy never felt very well in the morning, either, especially before breakfast, and once when he came downstairs and found that Muggs had moodily chewed up the morning paper he hit him in the face with a grapefruit and then jumped up on the dining room table, scattering dishes and silverware and spilling the coffee. Muggs' first free leap carried him all the way across the table and into a brass fire screen in front of the gas grate but he was back on his feet in a moment and in the end he got Roy and gave him a pretty vicious bite in the leg. Then he was all over it; he never bit anyone more than once at a time. Mother always mentioned that as an argument in his favor; she said he had a quick temper but that he didn't hold a grudge. She was forever defending him. I think she liked him because he wasn't well. "He's not strong," she would say, pityingly, but that was inaccurate; he may not have been well but he was terribly strong.

One time my mother went to the Chittenden Hotel to call on a woman mental healer who was lecturing in Columbus on the subject of "Harmonious Vibrations." She wanted to find out if it was possible to get harmonious vibrations into a dog. "He's a large tan-colored Airedale," mother explained. The woman said that she had never treated a dog but she advised my mother to hold the thought that he did not bite and would not bite. Mother was holding the thought the very next morning when Muggs got the iceman but she blamed that slip-up on the iceman. "If you didn't think he would bite you, he wouldn't," mother told him. He stomped out of the house in a terrible jangle of vibrations.

One morning when Muggs bit me slightly, more or less in passing, I reached down and grabbed his short stumpy tail and hoisted him into the air. It was a foolhardy thing to do and the last time I saw my mother, about six months ago, she said she didn't know what possessed me. I don't either, except that I was pretty mad. As long as I held the dog off the floor by his tail he couldn't get at me, but he twisted and jerked so, snarling all the time, that I realized I couldn't hold him that way very long. I carried him to the kitchen and flung him onto the floor and shut the door on him just as he crashed against it. But I forgot about the backstairs. Muggs went up the backstairs and down the frontstairs and had me cornered in the living room. I managed to get up onto the mantelpiece above the fireplace, but it gave way and came down with a tremendous crash throwing a large marble clock, several vases, and myself heavily to the floor. Muggs was so alarmed by the racket that when I picked myself up he had disappeared. We couldn't find him anywhere, although we whistled and shouted, until old Mrs. Detweiler called after dinner that night. Muggs had bitten her once, in the leg, and she came into the living room only after we assured her that Muggs had run away. She had just seated herself when, with a great growling and scratching of claws, Muggs emerged from under a davenport where he had been quietly hiding all the time, and bit her again. Mother examined the bite and put arnica on it and told Mrs. Detweiler that it was only a bruise. "He just bumped you," she said. But Mrs. Detweiler left the house in a nasty state of mind.

Lots of people reported our Airedale to the police but my father held a municipal office at the time and was on friendly terms with the police. Even so, the cops had been out a couple of times — once when Muggs bit Mrs. Rufus Sturtevant and again when he bit Lieutenant-Governor Malloy — but mother told them that it hadn't been Muggs' fault but the fault of the people who were bitten. "When he starts for them, they scream," she explained, "and that excites him." The cops suggested that it might be a good idea to tie the dog up, but mother said that it mortified him to be tied up and that he wouldn't eat when he was tied up.

Muggs at his meals was an unusual sight. Because of the fact that if you reached toward the floor he would bite you, we usually put his food plate on top of an old kitchen table with a bench alongside the table. Muggs would stand on the bench and eat. I remember that my mother's Uncle Horatio, who boasted that he was the third man up Missionary Ridge, was

THURBER

splutteringly indignant when he found out that we fed the dog on a table because we were afraid to put his plate on the floor. He said he wasn't afraid of any dog that ever lived and that he would put the dog's plate on the floor if we would give it to him. Roy said that if Uncle Horatio had fed Muggs on the ground just before the battle he would have been the first man up Missionary Ridge. Uncle Horatio was furious. "Bring him in! Bring him in now!" he shouted. "I'll feed the —— on the floor!" Roy was all for giving him a chance, but my father wouldn't hear of it. He said that Muggs had already been fed. "I'll feed him again!" bawled Uncle Horatio. We had quite a time quieting him.

In his last year Muggs used to spend practically all of his time outdoors. He didn't like to stay in the house for some reason or other — perhaps it held too many unpleasant memories for him. Anyway, it was hard to get him to come in and as a result the garbage man, the ice-man, and the laundryman wouldn't come near the house. We had to haul the garbage down to the corner, take the laundry out and bring it back, and meet the iceman a block from home. After this had gone on for some time we hit on an ingenious arrangement for getting the dog in the house so that we could lock him up while the gas meter was read, and so on. Muggs was afraid of only one thing, an electrical storm. Thunder and lightning frightened him out of his senses (I think he thought a storm had broken the day the mantelpiece fell). He would rush into the house and hide under a bed or in a clothes closet. So we fixed up a thunder machine out of a long narrow piece of sheet iron with a wooden handle on one end. Mother would shake this vigorously when she wanted to get Muggs into the house. It made an excellent imitation of thunder, but I suppose it was the most roundabout system for running a household that was ever devised. It took a lot out of mother.

A few months before Muggs died, he got to "seeing things." He would rise slowly from

the floor, growling low, and stalk stiff-legged and menacing toward nothing at all. Sometimes the Thing would be just a little to the right or left of a visitor. Once a Fuller Brush salesman got hysterics. Muggs came wandering into the room like Hamlet following his father's ghost. His eyes were fixed on a spot just to the left of the Fuller Brush man, who stood it until Muggs was about three slow, creeping paces from him. Then he shouted. Muggs wavered on past him into the hallway grumbling to himself but the Fuller man went on shouting. I think mother had to throw a pan of cold water on him before he stopped. That was the way she used to stop us boys when we got into fights.

Muggs died quite suddenly one night. Mother wanted to bury him in the family lot under a marble stone with some such inscription as "Flights of angels sing thee to thy rest" but we persuaded her it was against the law. In the end we just put up a smooth board above his grave along a lonely road. On the board I wrote with an indelible pencil "Cave Canem." Mother was quite pleased with the simple classic dignity of the old Latin epitaph.

splutteringly indignant when he found out that we fed the dog on a table because we were afraid to put his plate on the floor. He said he wasn't afraid of any dog that ever lived and that he would put the dog's plate on the floor if we would give it to him. Roy said that if Uncle Horatio had fed Muggs on the ground just before the battle he would have been the first man up Missionary Ridge. Uncle Horatio was furious. "Bring him in! Bring him in now!" he shouted. "I'll feed the —— on the floor!" Roy was all for giving him a chance, but my father wouldn't hear of it. He said that Muggs had already been fed. "I'll feed him again!" bawled Uncle Horatio. We had quite a time quieting him.

In his last year Muggs used to spend practically all of his time outdoors. He didn't like to stay in the house for some reason or other — perhaps it held too many unpleasant memories for him. Anyway, it was hard to get him to come in and as a result the garbage man, the iceman, and the laundryman wouldn't come near the house. We had to haul the garbage down to the corner, take the laundry out and bring it back, and meet the iceman a block from home. After this had gone on for some time we hit on an ingenious arrangement for getting the dog in the house so that we could lock him up while the gas meter was read, and so on. Muggs was afraid of only one thing, an electrical storm. Thunder and lightning frightened him out of his senses (I think he thought a storm had broken the day the mantelpiece fell). He would rush into the house and hide under a bed or in a clothes closet. So we fixed up a thunder machine out of a long narrow piece of sheet iron with a wooden handle on one end. Mother would shake this vigorously when she wanted to get Muggs into the house. It made an excellent imitation of thunder, but I suppose it was the most roundabout system for running a household that was ever devised. It took a lot out of mother.

A few months before Muggs died, he got to "seeing things." He would rise slowly from

85

the floor, growling low, and stalk stiff-legged and menacing toward nothing at all. Sometimes the Thing would be just a little to the right or left of a visitor. Once a Fuller Brush salesman got hysterics. Muggs came wandering into the room like Hamlet following his father's ghost. His eyes were fixed on a spot just to the left of the Fuller Brush man, who stood it until Muggs was about three slow, creeping paces from him. Then he shouted. Muggs wavered on past him into the hallway grumbling to himself but the Fuller man went on shouting. I think mother had to throw a pan of cold water on him before he stopped. That was the way she used to stop us boys when we got into fights.

Muggs died quite suddenly one night. Mother wanted to bury him in the family lot under a marble stone with some such inscription as "Flights of angels sing thee to thy rest" but we persuaded her it was against the law. In the end we just put up a smooth board above his grave along a lonely road. On the board I wrote with an indelible pencil "Cave Canem." Mother was quite pleased with the simple classic dignity of the old Latin epitaph.